Science & Math Rhymes 2 Help U

Alan Beech

ISBN: 0615895697
ISBN-13: 978-0615895697

To Audie

Introduction

I am a firm believer in learning stuff by rote, the slog that students, performers and the rest of us undergo. That said, sometimes a little lubrication in the form of a mnemonic helps. These rhymes are designed for occasional use as science and math aids, some may be of value only as an enjoyable way to learn some science facts. They differ from most science poems in that the help they give is more important than the poem, so meter or rhyme may sometimes suffer. I added comments or a summary of relevant science or math in front of most of the rhymes.

Rhyming mnemonics have a long history. “March winds and April showers, bring forth May flowers” is a short example. They also come in different guises. Some give lots of information but lots of words too, like “The Solar System”; others give the information in fewer words like “Pythagoras’ Theorem”. Another kind of mnemonic gives no direct information, just words to remind you of words or concepts, like “ Human Body Systems Reminder”. They are all grist for the mill. Wikipedia's entry for mnemonics states: "Academic study of the use of mnemonics has shown their effectiveness." This seems to apply to young and old people as well as short and long term memory.

This book contains 100 rhymes. It does not do justice to the huge amount of science, engineering, applied science and medical information that could be used to make up mnemonic rhymes. They are fun to compose and I hope to include more of them in a blog, coming soon.

Alan Beech 2013

ALPHABETIC INDEX

GENERAL SCIENCE

BIOLOGY

CHEMISTRY

PHYSICS

MATHEMATICS

GENERAL SCIENCE

1. Stalactites and Stalagmites

These deposits form when saturated calcium carbonate solutions drip slowly and some $CaCO_3$ precipitates out.

To the ceiling of a cave

The stalactite holds tight.

From the ground floor of a cave

The stalagmite grows height.

2. Planets of the Solar System

The sequence of planets in our Solar System from the Sun is Mercury, Venus, Earth, Mars, Jupiter, Saturn, Uranus, Neptune.

Eight little planets cool are we,
From the Sun Earth is number three.
Beautiful Venus next we see.
Nearest the Sun, tiny Mercury.

First on the right is Mars the red
Where the Roman war god bled.
Jupiter's next, huge blob of gas
Eight moons or more around it pass.

Nearly as big gassy Saturn see
A ball in a ring of ice debris.
Uranus and Neptune, so far away
Gassy & huge, little more to say.

3. Fat in Food

Small amounts are essential for hair, skin, cell membranes etc and vitamins a, d, e and k.

Fried foods and ice cream

So yummy they seem

Eat too much of those

You wind up adipose.

4. How big is a Billion?

The short numerical scale (billion = 10^9) is generally used by scientists and in English & Arabic speaking countries. The long numerical scale (billion = 10^{12}) is generally used in French, German, Dutch and Spanish speaking countries.

Don't confuse the zeroes to use

When you must write a billion line

Scientists, Brits and Yankees choose

Nine zeroes or ten to the nine.

A billion is more to other races

It's ten to the twelve in many places.

5. Miles, Kilometers and Cheetahs

Wild cheetahs have been clocked at 100 Km/Hr for short distances.

The speediest animals, cheetahs

Run at a hundred kilometers

(Or at sixty two miles) an hour

After game they want to devour.

6. Nautical Knot Speed

Knots are units of speed (distance traveled divided by time taken).

A knot, is not a lot

More than one mile an hour.

A seven knot speed by ship or by air

To just over eight miles an hour compare.

7. Metric Measures of Liquids

A cubic centimeter, within usual laboratory measurement limits, equals a milliliter. It is abbreviated to mL and pronounced "mill".

A cubic centimeter

Is also called a cc

Or else a milliliter

A mL to you and me.

8. Metric Prefixes & Equivalents

Giga is 10^9, mega is 10^6, kilo is 10^3 and hecto is 10^2.Centi is 10^{-2}, milli is 10^{-3}, micro is 10^{-6} and nano is 10^{-9}

.

A kilo of butter is pounds two point two

A kilo of meters is miles point six two.

Kilo's a thousand and giga's a billion

Milli's a thousandth and nano's a billionth.

Millionaires with megabucks cope

Microbes are viewed by a microscope.

Hecto's a hundred, mega's a million

Centi's a hundredth, micro's a millionth.

9. The Sun as a Compass

Just in case you get lost in a desert.

Facing the setting sun at night
North is always on your right
But it's not so at break of day
North turns you the other way.

10. Camels

D for one and B for two, Camel humps seen in a zoo.

Capital Bs have two bumps
Bactrian camels, two humps
Dromedaries one hump see
Like one curve on letter D.

11. Thunderstorm Safety

Lightning strikes from cloud to ground
May hit the tallest thing around
So don't stand underneath a tree
And don't swim in a lake or sea.

12. Thunderstorm Electricity

Thunder clouds that worry us
Are stormy cumulonimbus.
Protons to the cloud tops go
While electrons stay below.

These electrons as a band
Excite protons on the land
Proton plusses trail each cloud
Following the minus crowd.

Discharged as a lightning flash
With its mighty thunder crash
Cloud to cloud or cloud to ground
Making lots of light and sound.

BIOLOGY

13. Life characteristics List

Reminder

Movement, growth, sensation, respiration, nutrition, reproduction.

I am so I move

I grow and sensate,

Respire and I eat

And babies create.

14. Chromosomes in Mitosis

(Prophase, metaphase, anaphase, telophase. C's are Chromosomes).Mitosis is normal cell division, as in tissue repair. In prophase Chromosomes become visible, plus two centrosomes and spindles. The nuclear membrane disrupts and at metaphase centrosomes move to opposite sides and Chromosomes align along the midline. At anaphase Chromosomes divide and move toward opposite ends. In telophase nuclear envelopes form then the Chromosomes disappear.

We can first see the C's in phase pro-

They move to the midline in meta-

Toward their new ends C's in ana- go

In telo- you don't see the C's no mo'.

15. Darwin Tribute

Darwin's work, published in 1859, has been repeatedly vindicated since then. It provides the firm foundation for modern biology.

"On the Origin of Species"
Biology centerpiece is.
The theory of evolution
Was a science revolution.

16. Predator and Prey

Predator and prey may be interdependent, especially if the predator rarely seeks other prey. The arctic lynx and arctic hare are a good example.

Over-breeding predators
Decimate the prey
Leaving starving predators
Many waste away.

Fewer predators enable
The prey to over-breed
A predator dining table
To breed when they can feed.

17. Human Body Systems

Reminder

Respiratory, skeletal, muscular, endocrine, circulatory digestive, reproductive, nervous and excretory.

Lungs, bones, meat,

Steroids, heart, eat

Sex, fear, excrete.

18. Taxonomy

Taxonomy is the filing system for all living organisms.

It describes, identifies, names and classifies them

In taxonomy we collate
Flora and fauna in layers eight.

19. Taxonomic Classification of Humans

The eight layers are domain, kingdom, phylum, class, order, family, genus, species. For humans these are respectively eukarya, animal, chordate, mammal, primate, hominid, homo, sapiens. The first line of each couplet is nonsense.

My beau Jane is blue hairier

My domain is eukarya.

My income is minimal

My kingdom is animal.

My sly chum is your date

My phylum is chordate.

My ass is a camel

My class is a mammal.

My ardor says why wait

My order is primate.

My sanity is on the skid

My family is hominid.

My Venus is no mo'

My genus is homo.

My nieces are shapely hens

My species is sapiens.

20. Essential Amino Acids' Names

Our bodies make most of the amino acids that are the building blocks of proteins, but not the essential nine. Tryptophan, threonine, leucine, valine, phenylalanine, isoleucine, arginine, histidine, lysine.

Amino acids, essential nine

Eight of them in the family "ine"

(Pronounced in a way to rhyme with "mean")

Phenylalan- then leucine,

Threon-, isoleuc-, valine.

Three basic aa's in this scene

Arginine, histidine, lysine.

Amino acid tryptophan

(Not in the "ine" naming plan)

Is an essential mate

To all the other eight.

21. Amino acid Reactions

The generic structure of amino acids is acid-middlestuff-base, so they easily combine with each other, like holding hands

(eliminating a water molecule).

For amino acids it's hard to decide

Whether cations or anions to chase

The amino side needs an acid beside

And the acid side hunts for a base.

So amino acids, one, two or three

Joined into small peptides we see.

When hundreds of aa's joined are seen

They make a compound called protein.

22. Protein Digestion

Cells build their own proteins from the amino acids in blood plasma.

Proteins we consume in food

To amino acids are unglued.

To every cell they circulate

Where DNA proteins create.

23. Carbohydrates

Our bodies break carbohydrates down to CO_2 and water again, with the release of energy.

Plants make carbohydrates new

From water, sun and CO_2,

Sugars into starch compressed

Energy that we digest.

24. Photosynthesis

Plants absorb CO_2 from stomata, tiny openings on the underside of leaves. They draw in water through root hairs. Chloroplasts in leaf cells are the 'factories' where chemicals are made. Most of the reaction energy is from absorbing red and blue sunlight, green waves are reflected and give leaves their color.

All the things that people see
When looking at a plant or tree
Are made from water in the ground
And CO_2 from air around
Without any noise or sound.

Chlorophyll is catalyst
These reactions to assist.
It takes a lot of energy
Our Sun donates to them for free
To change a seed into a tree.

Photosynthetic product
Mainly sugars like sucrose,
From the leaves that make it
Along the phloem flows,
Throughout the plant it goes.

25. Ranking in Ecology

They are usually ranked the opposite way round, Individual, population, community, ecosystem, biome and biosphere.

All Earth's life is its biosphere

Biomes its largest division

Into ecosystems shear

Communities, next schism

Down to population

Then one in isolation.

26. Origin dates, Science Based.

For general knowledge, these are close enough estimates.

Life, Earth and Universe

Memorize their birth by verse.

Measured in billions of years

Life the baby 3 point 5 clears.

Earth at 5 for school is waiting

Universe 14 will soon be dating.

27. Big Bang

A substantial amount of scientific data supports the origin of the universe by a Big Bang about 13.8 billion years ago.

Lucky thirteen and point eight

Billion years ago (a rough date)

A Big Bang occurred

But nobody heard.

Universal creator.

(People turned up later).

28. Abiogenesis, Science-Based

Origin of Life

Scientists generally agree that life began on Earth about 3.5 billion years ago.
This relates to a popular theory of how life began.

In a shallow shelf one day
A compound simpler than DNA
Made a chemical like itself
With ingredients off the shelf.

Three and a half billion years ago
That chemical copycat did grow
First project initiation
Ancestor of creation.

29. Biological Eras

The Cenozoic Era began after a meteoric impact ended the reign of dinosaurs 65 million years ago (mya). The Mesozoic Era began 248 mya after the Great Extinction and the Paleozoic Era began 542 mya.

Longer version

The beginning of -ozoic era Pale
From five four two mya. did prevail.
Evolving species would flourish and fail.

The beginning of -ozoic era Mes
Two forty eight mya. (more or less).
When dinosaurs had great success.

The beginning of -ozoic era Cen
Was sixty five mya. that's when,
With mammals that would evolve to men.

Shorter version

Sixty five million years past

Cenozoic began with a blast.

The Mesozoic era date

Is mya two forty eight.

The era Paleozoic

Is five forty twoic.

30. Paleozoic Era Periods

Each line describes activity during the period named on the RHS.

Algae flourish in the seas	Cambrian
Fish but most invertebrate	Ordovician
Land invasion from the seas	Silurian
Plants on land proliferate	Devonian
Trees to fossils modify	Carboniferous
Big extinction many die.	Permian.

31. Birds as Dinosaurs

Most scientists accept that birds belong to class aves, the only surviving dinosaurs after the extinction 65.5 million years ago.

I never saw a dinosaur

Though I've been told

that they evolved

Into each bird

I've seen and heard.

32. Pharmacology

Pharmacology is the study of drugs and how our body deals with them. This part is called ADME.

Absorption its route to the bloodstream

Distribution through tissues extends

Metabolism is how it gets altered

Excretion is how action ends.

CHEMISTRY

33. Atoms & Molecules Defined

An atom is the smallest portion of an element that can exist alone or in combination. Molecules are the smallest portions of a substance that retain all its properties and are composed of one or more atoms.

Atoms are tiny building blocks

Most too reactive alone to exist

They join together as molecules

Particles stable enough to persist.

34. Element Defined

Elements are the simplest chemical substances that cannot be decomposed in a chemical reaction and that are made up of atoms all having the same number of protons

When the atoms in molecules

Are all the exact same kind

In a solid, liquid or gas

The name element is assigned.

35. Compounds Defined

A compound is a substance that can only be separated into two or more simpler substances by chemical reactions.

When different kinds of atoms combine

Their electrons may rearrange

The new compound has balanced charge

But electron loyalties change.

36. Lightest & Heaviest Elements

The first element in the Classical Periodic Table is hydrogen and the last is uranium (# 92). More than a dozen heavier elements have been created in labs, most of them in tiny amounts.

Atoms or elements, kinds ninety two

Plus some from laboratories, a few.

Hydrogen is the lightest weight's name

Uranium holds the heavyweight claim.

37. Ionic and Covalent Bonds

These are the two principal types of chemical bond between atoms. Ionic bonds are strong. Covalent bonds are weaker. Carbon forms covalent bonds.

By losing electrons
Atoms become cations.
By gaining electrons
Atoms become anions.

Anions to cations are bound
In every ionic compound

When two atoms A and B
Share electrons equally
A covalent bond we see.

38. Protons, Neutrons & Electrons Defined

The nucleus in the center of atoms holds positively charged protons and uncharged neutrons. These relatively heavy particles together define its atomic mass. The number of protons in the nucleus defines Its atomic number. The number of negatively charged electrons in orbits round the nucleus, generally equals the number of nuclear protons.

If we opened an atom to see inside

Three kinds of particles in it reside

Two kinds are bigger, the nuclear lot

Protons are positive, neutrons are not

Tiny electrons, those minus-charged e's

Fly round in orbits like buzzing of bees.

39. Stable Octet

Electron shells (energy levels or orbits) are outside atomic nuclei, # 3 (Lithium) to # 18 (Argon) need 8 electrons in their outer shell. Most chemical reactions involve the electrons in the outer shell.

Electrons circulate in a shell

It's the probable place they dwell.

As round nuclei they circulate

They need to fill a shell of eight.

40. Halogens React with Alkali Metals

F, Cl, Br and I

Need an e to fill a shell,

Metals Li, Na and K

Have an e that fits in well.

41. Isotopes

All the atoms of an element have the same number of protons, its atomic number. The number of neutrons in atoms of an element may vary. Each variant is called an isotope. An element's relative atomic mass is an average of masses of its isotopes.

In all the atoms with a given name.
The number of protons is the same.
With neutron variance we must cope
And call each one an isotope.

42. Cations

Cations are atoms short of electrons so they carry a positive charge e.g.. Na^+, K^+, H^+. In batteries or electrolysis they move to the cathode.

Is a lion like a cat?

I'm not certain about that.

But I'm positive that positive cations

Are not in any way similar to lions.

43. Halogen Names

Don't mispronounce iodine.

First four halogens rhyme with bean

Fluorine, chlorine, bromine, iodine.

44. Alkali Metals & Halogens

Atoms of fluorine, chlorine, bromine and iodine need one electron to fill their outer shell. Atoms of elements lithium, sodium and potassium each have one electron in their outer shells. As a yenta would say, it's a perfect match.

Lithium, sodium and potassium

Are metals, reactive and soft,

But cations (positive) they become

When one electron is offed.

Sodium metal and gas chlorine

Combine together in a flash

Lots of heat and light is seen

And sodium chloride as an ash.

45. Acids in Food

Vinegar is 5-8% acetic acid in water plus other trace substances. Lemonade contains 0.1-0.8% citric acid plus sugar etc. Colas generally contain dilute phosphoric acid.

Lots of acids are nasty

But some when diluted are nice.

Acetic acid in vinegar,

Lemonade (citric) with ice.

46. Concentrated Mineral Acids

Treat these chemicals with respect. They attack organic material (like skin) in concentrated form. Diluted enough they are innocuous.

Hydrochlor<u>ic</u> and nitr<u>ic</u>

Sulfur<u>ic</u> and phosphor<u>ic</u>.

<u>Icky</u> acids you may see

In a chemist's laboratory.

47. Reaction of Acid with Base

Acid + base = salt + water

If the reactants are acid and base

Neutralization will take place

H and hydroxyl ions bind

A salt and water products find.

48. Reaction of Acid with Alcohol

Acid + alcohol = Ester + water

When alcohol and acid react

H and OH ions interact

Alkyls with anions slowly bind

Products esters and water find.

49. Carboxylic Acids

For carboxylic acids, look,

For a formula with a HOOC-

But if that doesn't do

Instead look for a -COOH.

50. Ethanoic acid

The word "vinegar" comes from the Old French word "vinaigre" meaning sour wine.

Ethanoic acid is similar

To acetic acid in vinegar.

Also called methyl-COOH

By me and you.

If oxygen gets in the brew

Wine turns into methyl-COOH.

(Et-OH becomes Me-COOH)

51. Ethyl Ethanoate

(Ethanoic acid, ethyl ester).

Students often have difficulty in assigning the correct formula of an ester like this to its name.

When chemists create

Ethyl eth-an-o-ate

They need to glue

Some methyl-COOH

(Less H_2O)

With ethyl-OH.

Me-CO-OEt

Is what they get.

(I realize that the word 'glue' is wrong

'React' doesn’t rhyme and it's too long).

52. Avogadro Number and a Mole

This is the number of atoms in 12 grams of carbon-12,called a mole. It equals the number of molecules in the formula weight of a chemical in grams.

Avogadro knew

A mole would always be

Six point oh two two

Times ten to twenty three.

53. Molar Solution

The molecular weight of a compound in grams (formula weight) is one mole. When a mole of a compound is dissolved in water and made up to a thousand mL (one liter) it is a molar solution.

Weigh out in grams the formula weight

In distilled water then dissipate

Make to a liter with distillate

A molar solution you create.

PHYSICS

54. Newton's First Law

Newton's First Law of Motion states: Every body continues in a state of rest or of uniform motion in a straight line unless it is acted upon by an externally impressed force.

Newton said things will

Always stay quite still

Or at constant velocity

If they're already moving free

Unless an outside force

Modifies that course.

55. Newton's Second Law

Acceleration is produced when a force acts on a mass. The greater the mass, the greater the force needed.

Mass times acceleration
To force an equal relation.
In equation form we say
f = m times a.

56. Newton's Third Law

To every action there is an equal and opposite reaction.

Each action has a sequel

Opposite and equal.

57. Mass and Weight

Bathroom scales measure how much gravity attracts your mass to Earth. On the Moon they would show you weighing just over 16 pounds for each 100 lb they show now. Doctor's scales with counterbalances measure mass, so would show the same result on Moon or Earth.

Mass is the same
Any place you name
In outer space
Or any place.

Your weight
At this location
Is mass times the rate
You accelerate
By gravitation.

58. Favorite Moments

The moment of a force is the force multiplied by the distance of its point of application from the fulcrum.

The book you just opened,

The faucet you turned,

The hoop you set rolling,

The ice-cream you churned,

These four examples of moments, you learn,

Are forces applied to make something turn.

59. The Inverse Square Law

The intensity of illumination at a point from a source decreases in proportion to the square of its distance from the source ($I \alpha\ 1/distance^2$)

From it's source light has a propensity

To quickly decrease in intensity

In proportion to the square

Of its distance to anywhere.

60. The Law of Gravitation

Newton's Law of Universal Gravitation is related to the inverse square law. Every body attracts every other body with a force proportional to the product of their masses and inversely proportional to the square of their distance apart. The proportionality constant is called G.

$F = (Gm_1m_2)/r^2$

The attracting force of gravitation

On the left side of the equation

Is product of both masses and big G

Over squared (how far apart they be).

61. Big G

Big G is $6.674/10^8$. Its units are length in cm/(mass in grams) x (time in seconds)^2. Little g is 32 feet/(second)^2 or 981 cm/(second)^2.

Acceleration due to Earth's gravity

Is commonly written as little g

It is not a constant universally

That one is usually called big G.

62. Friction in Driving and Sky Diving

Terminal velocity from free falling is reached when the frictional resistance of the air equals your rate of acceleration.

Air friction is every place

Unless we are in outer space.

It slows us down when fast we drive

And limits speed in a sky dive.

63. Braking Friction

Brakes apply friction

To a car's traction

They slow the action.

This isn't fiction.

64. Density

In laboratories we usually measure density in grams per cubic centimeter (g/cm^3).Examples are water = 1, cork = 0.25, glass 2.6, iron = 7.8, gold = 19.3. In industry, density is measured in kilograms per cubic meter. The conversion factor is 1000 e.g. Iron = $7800kg/m^3$.

Mass per unit volume

Defines the density

Or mathematically

M over V is D.

A volume of water

One mL or one cc

Its mass is one gram

And one its density.

65. Specific Gravity (SG)

SG = D_{liq}/D_{water} .but as D_{water} = $1g/cm^3$ the units cancel, so SG has no units.

Hydrometer readings show

Density as a ratio

To density of H_2O.

Though the number is the same

Specific gravity is its name.

It is now a ratio, so all of the units go.

66. Velocity

Velocity is a vector quantity. It measures the rate that position changes, so the direction is part of the measurement.

If things move straight from A to B

Reporting their direction,

Speed then equals velocity

Along their course selection.

67. Fumes

Fumes and vapors are droplets of a liquid or solid finely dispersed in the air.

A fume has no volume,

It will fill the room.

Some per-sistent fumes,

Are made by per-fumes.

68. States of Matter

Solids have a fixed volume and shape. Liquids have a fixed volume but adopt the shape of their container. Gases adopt the volume and shape of their container.

When molecules are cold
They bond up close together,
Like we keep warm in wintry weather.
That state we call a solid.

When it gets a little warmer
Molecules don't stay so near,
They change bonds fast but still adhere.
That state we call a liquid.

When molecules get warmer still
Like birds up in the sky,
They break the family bonds and fly.
That state we call a gas.

69. Heat and Temperature

Temperature defines the heat energy of a body or system. The absolute zero is -273.2° Celsius.

Cold and warm we know for sure

Are measured by the temperature.

As heat out from a system flows

All molecular movement slows.

Absolute zero by Celsius decree

Is minus two hundred and seventy three.

70. Temperature Scales

Using the Celsius scale water has F. Pt 0° C and B. Pt 100° C. By the Fahrenheit scale water has F. Pt 32° F and B. Pt. 212 °F, so there are 9 degrees F for every 5 degrees C The conversion factor is 5/9 (Don't forget the 32° F)

Boiling to freezing Fahrenheit sees

As a hundred and eighty tiny degrees.

For the same heat loss Celsius sees

Intervals of one hundred degrees.

71. Speed (velocity) of Light

Velocity and speed in a straight line are numerically equal. Light moves at 186,000 miles a second or 700 million miles an hour. Astronomical distances are measured in light years (distance light travels in a year).

We are ninety three million miles

About eight minutes from the sun,

Traveling at the speed of light

The fastest that anything's done.

72. Electricity

Electricity, type of energy,

Conveyed by electron jostle.

Electrons do not move very far

But its current speed is colossal.

73. Conduction Heat Transfer

If you touch a hot stove, heat transfers to your skin by conduction.

Heat increases molecular vibration

In metals, a close-packed situation.

The neighbors vibrate, a production

Called heat transfer by conduction.

74. Convection Heat Transfer

When molecules are warmed they vibrate more and expand so their density decreases. This is why warmed liquids and gases rise. When they cool, they contract, density increases and they fall. This circulation is called convection.

Heat a gas or liquid, up by convection

It will always move, in an upward direction.

75. Radiation Heat Transfer

Infra red rays carry heat from the sun (but ultra violet rays cause a sunburn).

Heat by radiation

Electromagnetic vibration.

76. Wave Velocity Equation

Velocity = frequency x wavelength. For EM waves $C = \nu\lambda$

The product of wavelength and frequency

Of any old wave is velocity.

77. Transverse Waves Described

EM and seashore waves are transverse

Waves that go up then reverse

Are the kind we call transverse.

78. Compression Waves Described

Sound is transmitted by compression or longitudinal waves.

Every verbal expression

Evokes waves of compression.

79. About Electromagnetic Rays

Visible light is the example, but this applies to all Em rays.

Each EM particle or ray

Behaves in a similar way

Electromagnetic rays in fact

Can focus, reflect and refract.

Focus

To a focus rays converge

From a focus they diverge.

Reflection

Beams of reflected and incident light

make equal angles to a normal upright.

Refraction

When beams of light pass from air into glass

Refracted beams skew toward normals new.

80. Photons

Photons are difficult to understand. Sometimes they behave as particles and sometimes waves. They represent force energy and have no resting mass. All electromagnetic waves are photons. As their wavelength decreases their frequency increases. The greater the frequency of the photons the greater is their energy and penetrating ability.

Photons like energy cross dressers behave

Sometimes they're particle and other times wave

Although they all move at the same speed as light

Their frequency measures how much they excite.

80a. The Electromagnetic Spectrum

The EM spectrum is a continuum from gamma rays to short x rays to long x rays to short UV to long UV to visible light (VIBGYOR) to short IR to long IR to short radio/media to long radio/media.

81. Gamma Rays

Wavelength smallest but energy a whammer

Waves from radioactive stuff called gamma.

82. X Rays

Fractures by x-rays are diagnosed

Their tiny wavelengths penetrate most.

83. UV Rays

Ultra violet waves called UV

Shorter than violet colors you see.

84. Visible Rays

Violet waves view, then to indigo go,
Blue and then green are next in a row.
Yellows like lemons to oranges change,
Red, longest waves in the visible range.

85. Infra-Red Rays

Longer than visible waves infra-red
Eyes cannot see but we feel heat instead.

86. Media & Radio Rays

The longest EM waves we know
Carry media messages and radio.

87. Radioactive Products

In chemical reactions the nuclei of atoms do not change. The electrons rearrange but the nuclei and identities of participating elements stay the same. Radioactive atoms are different. They have unstable nuclei. When a nucleus decomposes, alpha, beta or gamma radiation may evolve and a different element is formed.

Alpha-lumps positive

Be-lectrons negative

Gamma rays no charge give.

88. Alpha Emanation

Particles alpha, from atoms decayed

Of two protons and two neutrons made.

Though they may not penetrate much

It's death for every cell they touch.

89. Beta Emanation

Beta with velocity great
More than alpha can penetrate
Electrons carry negative charge
Harm and ionize where they barge.

90. Gamma Emanation

Gamma, an energy radiation
Has the maximum penetration.
Exposure kills but focused see
Gamma knives in surgery.

MATHEMATICS

91. Trig Ratios

Sine = opposite/hypotenuse, abbrev. Sin = opp/hyp.

Cosine = adjacent/hypotenuse, abbrev. Cos = adj/hyp.

Tangent = opposite/adjacent, abbrev. Tan = opp/adj.

Sin occurs if an opp
Hops over a hypotenuse.

A cos célèbre may occur
If adjacent should prefer
to hop over a hypotenuse.

If an opp in a ménage
Should hop over an adj
A perfect tan ensues.

92. Circle

Diameter

The diameter D of a circle is a chord or straight line passing through its middle.

How did Dee cut the pie?

Can you solve the riddle?

D (diameter) cut the pie

Straight across the middle.

Circumference

The Greek letter π (pron. Pie), spelt pi is defined as the ratio of the circumference of a circle to its diameter. Therefore the circumference of a circle is πd.

The distance round a pie
Is always d times π
It's not a coincidence
It is a circumference.

Area

The area of a circle is πr^2 where radius $r = d/2$.

I was scared of π(r squared).
But an area is less scarier.

93. Triangle

Equilateral

In equilateral triangles all the angles are 60° .

Three sides and three angles the same

Has an equilateral name.

Isosceles

Isosceles triangles have two equal sides and two equal angles.

For triangles isosceles

Two sides of equal length one sees.

Scalene

Scalene triangles have 3 different length sides and 3 different angles.

When three unequal sides are seen

The triangles are called scalene.

94. Sum of Angles of a triangle

The three angles of a triangle always add up to 180° .

A triangle's three angular knees

Add up to a hundred and eighty degrees.

95. Right Angled Triangle

Right angled triangles have one angle of 90° so they can't be equilateral. They are either isosceles or scalene.

A right triangle, if you please

Has one angle of ninety degrees.

96. Which Side is the Hypotenuse?

In a right angled triangle the hypotenuse is always opposite the 90° angle.

The ninety degree angle

Of a right angle triangle,

From a distance views

The hypotenuse.

97. The Theorem of Pythagoras

A square on the hypotenuse is equal in area to the sum of the squares on the other two sides.

Pythagoras said that a square

On a hypotenuse anywhere

Of a right triangle coincides

With the sum of squares on the other two sides.

98. The Theorem of Pythagoras Extended

This is college stuff. In any triangle, if the lengths of sides a and b and angle θ between them are known, then $c^2 = a^2 + b^2 - 2ab\cos\theta$.

In any triangle the side C squared

Is equal to A squared plus B squared

Less two AB cos the angle enclosed

(Something else Pythagoras proposed).

99. Quadratic Equation Solution

When $ax^2 + bx + c = 0$ then $x = [-b \pm \sqrt{(b^2 - 4ac)}]/2a$

X in quadratics compute

Minus b plus/minus square root

(b squared minus four ac

In the square root sign see)

Everything now underlay

By dividing it by 2a.

100. The Equations of Motion

The equations of motion apply to things that move in a straight line with constant acceleration. Distance is d or s, initial velocity v_i or u, final velocity v_f or v. Most people agree on the abbreviations a for acceleration and t for time taken.

Final Velocity Missing

$d = v_i t + ½ at^2$ or $s = ut + ½ at^2$

Distance is time times initial velocity

But only when this product is shared

With half the product of ‘a’ and ‘t’ squared.

Time Missing

$v_f^2 = v_i^2 + 2ad$ or $v^2 = u^2 + 2as$

Final velocity when it’s squared

Equals initial velocity squared

With twice distance times ‘a’ paired.

Distance Missing

$v_f = v_i + at$ or $v = u + at$

The initial velocity

and acceleration times ‘t’.

Make the final velocity.

Acceleration Missing

$d = (v_i + v_f)t/2$ or $s = (u + v)t/2$

Initial plus final velocity is tied

Then by half time taken is multiplied

To find the distance of the ride.

About the Author

Alan Beech grew up in England and received a B. Sc. Special degree from the University of London in chemistry with physics, math and biology minors. In the United States he earned a Ph. D. in pharmacology at the U of MD School of Medicine. He has worked in the pharmaceutical industry and taught in medical school, pharmacy school, community college and high school. He is an amateur actor, hippie and poet, now retired.

Notes

Notes

www.ingramcontent.com/pod-product-compliance
Lightning Source LLC
LaVergne TN
LVHW021543080426
835509LV00019B/2811
9780615895697